The Backwards Year

Other Books by Joe Weil

What Remains (Nightshade Books)

Painting the Christmas Trees (Texas Review Press)

The Plumber's Apprentice (NYQ Books)

West of Home (with Emily Vogel, Blast Press)

The Great Grandmother Light (NYQ Books)

A Night in Duluth (NYQ Books)

The Backwards Year

Poems

Joe Weil

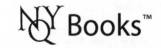

The New York Quarterly Foundation, Inc.
Beacon, New York

NYQ Books™ is an imprint of The New York Quarterly Foundation, Inc.

The New York Quarterly Foundation, Inc.
P. O. Box 470
Beacon, NY 12508

www.nyq.org

First Edition

Set in New Baskerville

Layout by Raymond P. Hammond

Cover Design by Raymond P. Hammond

Cover Illustration: "Family Wading in River", 19" x 25" gouache on paper by Linda Hillringhouse, 2005 https://lindahillringhouse.zenfolio.com

Library of Congress Control Number: 2020931923

ISBN: 978-1-63045-066-3

In memory of my brothers,
John and Peter.

Author's Note

Some of these poems have appeared in present or slightly different form in *Tiferet, Paterson Literary Review, Big Hammer, Journal of New Jersey Poets, Steve* (in Both English and in Italian translation), and various anthologies, including *Like Light: 25 Years of Poetry and prose* by Bright Hill Press, and *Misrepresented People: Poetic Responses to Trump's America*'s an anthology by NYQ Books. I am grateful to all those who supported my poetry over the years, especially Emily Vogel. I dedicate the book to my late brothers John and Peter Weil and to the memory of my friend, Joe Salerno.

—*Joe Weil, more or less*

CONTENTS

Part Two: A Word to the Wise

Part Three: Post-Pastoral

Postlude: A Little Hope

The Backwards Year

The Backwards Year

an Invocation

As naked as I came
Beyond all blight and blame
I crash through months, weeks, years
Aunt Kay with pruning shears
Goes clip clip as I drop
some sixty years, then stop
just short of my ma's womb
or should I say the tomb?
Cheap verities of time
Bore most men when they rhyme.
And I admit this trick
Seems bad arithmetic.
So to one year I'll stick
And backwards go my way
The living and the dead
will feel my gentle tread
If gentle's what I do
Moonwalking towards adieu
Yes, backwards then we'll go
From snow to falling snow.

Part One: The River in Reverse

Mourning Dove

This morning my daughter Clare
clung and wouldn't let go
her legs wrapped around my waist
and her arms pressed to my neck.
I didn't mind wearing her.
If I could wear Clare the rest of my life
well, then so be it.
But we heard the bus up the hill
then saw it riding down: all yellow
and black, putting forth its stop signs
like some giant black-eyed Susan
into which my little bee climbed
and was gone, the doors closing
behind her, leaving me bare foot
against cold walk and colder lawn.
The silence after she'd been swallowed up
was filled with the warmth of her
freshly pulled from me—still leaving
an impress, like a hat you continue to
wear long after it's been fully doffed.
That's when I heard them—the mourning
doves, three perched on the telephone
wires. Are they telephone wires?
One still sleeping with its tiny head
dropped into its chest, but the others
cooed their sad lament, as if to say
there is no end to coming and going and
either becomes the same, after you've
been coming and going long enough
to start to feel the death in things—
not of, but in, and all the coming
is going and all the going is coming
and the bus is a big Black Eyed Susan
and the nape of your daughter's neck
escapes a final kiss as she mounts

17

the stairs, encouraged by the aid.
Good bye! And hiss of the hydraulic
doors, and then you're here alone
feet numb, listening to the Mourning doves,
those subdued and well-dressed
pigeons, hunted in other parts of the country
to the tune of up to 70 million birds,
So in demand that ideal seed—their
favorite—is planted for the slaughter.
And you wonder what's been planted for your
five-year-old daughter. Who waits at the
top of the stairs and at the end?
At two she began imitating the mourning doves
that cooed outside her bedroom window
at dawn and dusk. Took you awhile to know
she was learning their song. She mimics
the mourning dove and the jay. They were
the first birds in her cradle song.
And now the house is empty. There's a dead
Chipmunk left by your cat to let you know
he offers his share to the larder.
The cat is better now at killing—no marks,
the Chipmunk's beautiful. The song
of the Mourning dove is inside you—
the press of your daughter still against your
chest. You almost coo. Instead you
turn the chipmunk with a hoe, toss him
into the shrubbery. They can dig thirty foot
burrows under your house, destroy the
foundations. Good for them!
The Mourning Dove is not a
peaceful bird. Peace is a construct
dove has come to symbolize. It's fierce at
bird feeders, a bully to Sparrows
When the dove drinks, it does not lift its

head, but sucks the water in like nectar, sips
its own reflection. When it flees the scene
it makes a high tea kettle whistle
with its wings—a quick flying bird.
My Clare swallows deep and makes the
grieving sound—the gulping coo she's
heard all her life. She is "non-verbal,"
"On the spectrum." Sometimes she clings
so fiercely, at others she pushes me away.
She likes to drum with her hands on my head
It hurts. The dove on over cast days, in
a light rain, appears to be the color of rain—
not so much transparent or translucent, as
the subtlest, leeched pussy willow grey.
My daughter too is sometimes on the verge
of disappearing—rain child with a rain dove coo:
a grey I wear in the bright yellow, the black-eyed
Susan of my life. This grief I can bear.
Because a long time ago I learned love does
not refuse the weight that plants it
deep, the weight of the snow on
rods of Forsythia, that causes the rods to bloom,
the weight of my daughter so tight against
my chest, and above me, the doves
crying, the voice heard throughout the land.

The Hawk and Its Shadow

We begin with snow packed hard against a pin oak that has
blocked the sun—

    A blue snow

You wouldn't notice except something has stirred there—a
rabbit hunkering down

    In fear of

A goshawk. The way the Jays are screeching out their own
name, ten jays like a throng.

    it must be

A hawk. And the rabbit is always afraid, always and no
wonder considering how often it must be

    Devoured

By everything that is hungry with claws and jaws and talons
and beaks to rend—everything

    Wandering these suburbs

Six deer in the driveway, two weeks past the rut, steam rising
from what little snow is

    Left alone in the shadow line of trees and houses

This piebald earth, the ground sodden until next freeze,
The rabbit twitches. The jays keep

    Chasing both the hawk and its shadow.

Reversal

December 2017

The river, too full of itself,
Engorged with a 40-day rain
Runs in reverse, flees from the sea,
The sea which might have absolved it,
The ocean checks its watch and
Noting the river has stood it up,
retreats a mile, even ten miles out,
Leaving detritus of horse shoe crabs
mollusks, drift wood, penny loafers,
condoms, needles from that Hospital
by the bay, doll's heads, the half rotten
corpses of gulls, a man in a brown suit,
bloated, yet still clutching a pin wheel.
I take the pin wheel from his swollen
Fingers. The wind makes it spin.
The man rises and tells me he is
Joe and works for the government.
Only he has forgotten which one.
I show him a map of the world
Which I keep at hand, just in case.
And he says: *There it is! Estonia!*
When he walks, the sea in his shoes
Makes a squishing noise.
The pin wheel is for his daughter
Sophia, which means wisdom.
He begins to cry. Perhaps she's dead.
Perhaps he lost her to whatever
Lack of vision made him walk across
Thousands of miles of sea
I say *call to the river. Listen*
And the dead will rise. There is a Shofar
for all grief. All of us soaked in losses
And the spirit blows its horn.
He shouts Sophia as the river runs back

21

Down through the vast hills and onto the
Plains. The sea runs even faster to embrace it.
Everything is prodigal. All that I love
Has welled up and reversed its flow.

A True Dynamic

After Braque

The wounds have turned into light
at their edges, whole villages have settled.
Men in polo shirts peer down
into their chasms
and joke about lost golf balls.

The objects on tables accept
their new-found destiny: apples, and
fish, compasses and
grapes have assumed
a true dynamic

The table tilts and, at times, curves

What breaks, at the moment
of fracturing, leaves space
and movement into and out of time.

Only then can things be whole,
perceived for what they are:

I have made a great discovery
I no longer believe in anything.
The cue ball does not exist.
The eight ball does not exist,
only the sound of one kissing
the other, and the trajectory of that
collision: left side corner pocket exists.

Once the ball has dropped,
I no longer exist except as a stick

laid slantwise on the table over an expanse of
green felt, or is it grass? We began
on a savannah with an occasional hill
or tree from which to peer
to see what dangers or what meal might be
approaching.

What approaches now? The grapes
have no sheen on them, no gloss,
the apple has divorced its own shadow

which now rises elsewhere.
Independent of whatever cast it:

The painting is finished when the idea
has disappeared: one halibut,
one opera advertisement,
a violin bending like a swooning
poet, a poet transformed into a
bowl of grapes, one mallard
two large cheeses, a few lemons,

and what could it all mean?
The wound has turned into light.
The men in their polo shirts
have all gone home to bed.
The jokes have stopped,
and now the golf balls glow
fluorescent in the dark: thousands
upon thousands, and mirror

the night sky—each decomposing the other's
repertoire of ghosts
the truth exists and only the lies are invented
or perhaps it is the other way around.

The Skull at the End of the Driveway

There was a skull
at the end of my driveway—
a little bird's skull
the wind had leeched
of everything but bone

And I placed it on my index finger
looking at it from
all angles, admiring its

delicacy, its efficient
shapeliness, nothing

either homely or
wasted, a whistle
for wind. and I blew against

my finger, heard,
the hollow sound,
its intimate music. I was
alone, and the
first stars were

coming out above
the neighbor's house.
How lucky I was, how
blessed that all things
were as simple as they were
and no simpler.

Poem to Myself

When the stuff you have on the wall
is just stuff you have on the wall
which you hardly look at at all and
when you're phone is 9 thousand indie
bands on shuffle, and you're in debt
and your job is like some old Harold Lloyd
Film, with Harold dangling off a skyscraper
and you realize you're too smart for the
fake smart people who don't even
know who Harold Lloyd is, and too dumb
for the truly smart people who know, but who
manage to handle knowledge like
something to which they'd flip the bird,
well then—maybe you can stare at a grey
cat and say: *I wish I were dead. I really want*
to die right now. I want to cut my wrists
and screw everyone, but you don't because
you're too old not to know emotions only
last for a long time if you're clinically depressed,
and there's drugs for that. Six hours from now
someone might say something that
makes you laugh. It's not enough, but, for now
it'll do. Harold Lloyd's ghost is alive and well
thanks to the Smithsonian. There are people
who care and care deeply about shit
that doesn't just hang or repeat itself every
200 songs. You would like to meet one of
those people. Once you stared at a painting
for seven hours. You weren't high or drunk
and the painter wasn't even famous.
You didn't need to buy it. It stayed in your
memory. If you close your eyes now
it will reappear. Ignore the tears that are massing
like some evil horde at the borders of your retinas.
You are the person you want to meet. and

everyone has been a cock block, an impediment
It is hard to meet yourself. You believe all the
rumors spread about you. You have fallen into
the wrong kind of faith—one where no one
'worships.' Get up, fuck face, gird your loins
You are someone who stared at a painting for
seven hours. They can take away your job, your
children, your house, everything they think makes
you sort of worthwhile. But you know the young
boy who stared. he isn't going anywhere. Put your
hands on his shoulders, touch him, feel his body shake
because he is so afraid, stare with him, cry with
him. He's the one who will save you.

What We Need to Live

I still get junk mail for my Ma
from the Maryknoll fathers,
41 years after her death.

I always include them in the change
of address. After all no one
who gets junk mail

is ever *really dead.* I have
my book bag from 4th grade,
filled with wrinkled homework

and the first story I ever wrote
told by a narrator who
admits at the end that he always

lies when he's drunk (and he's drunk).
If I am ever cremated, I want
my ashes in that book bag, and

fuck the church who says
sacred ground, which really means
give us ten thousand bucks.

The book bag is puce green
I used to belly flop on it
on the ice of the Acme parking lot.

I fended off six older kids
who thought I might
have money by swinging

it wildly, eyes clenched.
So much has been lost in my life—
to homelessness, to my own

innate disarray. What I have managed
to keep, if only as a story told
sober, told with the full

weight and knowledge of my being
is what keeps me alive,
keeps me praying with my

daughter Clare when she
can't sleep, and Hail Mary
full of grace becomes her lullaby.

I want to show her
Her grandmother's name on
the junk mail, the smiling

Maryknolls—fathers who
haven't gotten a dime out of me
in 41 years: Clare, Clare

Clare on the envelope, Clare in her
bed., Clare which means light
but reminds me of Clay

and means earth to me, the ground
where I take off my sandals;
Ground set apart. Arc of my life.

From Clare to Clare, from
light to earth I'll go. No one
knows what sacred ground is

until they have stumbled on it.
Grace for me has always been
a kind of stumbling.

What do I know of walking straight
except into walls? I am still swinging
that book bag with all my might,
eyes clenched—my body a gathering wind.

Homage to the English House Sparrow

All the song birds
have fallen to paws
and more, importantly, jaws

of someone's adorable kitty:
Orioles have lost their elms
and no longer frequent the city

And since we like things so clean
so neat, so utterly symmetrical,
we've turned the world into green

pool tables of overly fertilized lawns—
each golf course an eco-disaster
the thickets, and waste places

(which, perish the thought, are a mess)
are bulldozed and replaced by
decorative cabbages and ornamental

grass—nothing out of order, nothing that
can feed a single wild thought:
a series of circles, triangles and squares

all for the fast food franchises and the
Wells Fargo banks, the tanning salons
and the Sam's Clubs

and thanks to landscapers, not a single
dead leaf ever hops the border,
the whole thing saying to Butterfly

as well as Purple finch, Warbler,
as well as Rufous Towhee: *Go away,*
Go away!

We annihilated the Passenger
pigeon for hats (and for
slave food), and the American

Chestnut soon went down with
them, but the
English House Sparrows, the sparrows

are alive and well and living at Lowe's!
You can see them chirping happily amid
the lawnmowers, and the plumbing supplies

they fill every bush
from San Diego to Maine and annoy you
while you try to eat your Chilean sea bass

at some outdoor cafe, and they love cement
and circles, and triangles and squares
as much as we do. On the golf courses, they're

food for the red-tailed Hawks, but mostly
they just gather in winter bushes and in the eaves
of roofs, in parking lots, gas stations, Subways,

having replaced Emily Dickinson's
House wren and the purple martins.
In Manhattan, the Peregrine falcon

clips them from 400 feet of sky.
They die, and they die, and they die
only to rise yet again to flitter and chirp

and keep up their Sparrow patois
so much so that my grandmother
would cry out in despair when we were loud

"Jesus, Mary and Joseph! You're a bush full
of Sparrows!"
These birds dressed in the color of soot

and dung, the dirty buff of unwashed cars
survivors: the children of our urban sprawl
the beneficiaries of our slaughter.

A Sort of Ars Poetica

If you don't care that a basketball
sounds different being dribbled on a sidewalk in December
than it does in May, and that it *REALLY*
sounds different if the dribbler is alone
and if you are not
even now seeing the kid in the purple wind breaker too
slight for Winter
and if you don't know he sleeps sometimes
in that jacket
because it's a Lakers jacket—a cheap knock off
but his, all his and perhaps all that is his
beyond the ball and the gloaming,
if you don't care because you are busy
learning something from a master at some retreat
then read no further.
You're right. I know nothing about poetry

The Failure to Be Jade

Poems that have no tricks in them
are fairly boring
and those with too many tricks are boring too
and since we have been cool since Byron
and bored since the French court of (pick a date)
you'd think both tricks and the absence of tricks
would delight us (and they do).
I was winterizing all my voices when I looked at
the peeled paint—right there where your
neck is acutest at its vanishing.
I was dead to living poets.
I was dead to sneakers that made a personal statement.
I was dead to people who were trying to punish me
via outrage and seances.
I was dead from knowing this was an example of anaphora.
written
due to a total lack of sleep.
I didn't want to thank the editors since I hadn't
sent them any work.
I wanted to disappear into my Facebook profile
which was looking more and more like Hitchcock's.
No one said thank you and then someone did
and my heart started crumbling like ancient parchment.
I forgave the ground because it was touched
by the shoes of someone who meant
it: there were words in Syrian and Armenian and ancient
Sanskrit and all of them comprised this sentence.
Lack of sleep will make you write the sort of poems
that don't "move" the already too easily moved.
And then there are those who, though skinny, are immovable
impervious—jaded I suppose in the worst sense.
I have tried to be jaded. I have turned green with
trying. There is a white jade, known as Sheep fat jade
(I learned that from a student). It made me think of

the heavy arms of my aunts, all of whom would make
large plates of baked lima beans with bacon.
I see them laughing in the sun, their arms jiggling.
They're all dead, and perhaps it was the lima beans that did it.
They were happy with each other in the yard,
laughing and smoking pall mall reds.
I am seriously in love with the exact sort of people
most of the artsy types despise:
they were just about to offer me some jello cake
but then the poem whisked them back into their graves
I am left with all the other kinds of people who are
so smart, so damned smart, so god awful smart, So—
The French court, a facsimile on PBS, ten thousand
smart folks all out smarting each other.
One radiant poet who understands the lima beans
writes that she still has a report card
where I wrote "verbal smoke screen and emotional distance"
She said I was right, and I was right, but this poem, too, is
all smoke and yet, the Aunts, too, are not enough
though I stand a stout clumsy boy, sort of an uglier
Elton John,
in a striped polo shirt
in their cool shadows on the purple grass, smiling for a long lost
photo—though I loved every last—limited—non-artsy—
bright—sarcastic—cig—in—the—mouth one of them:
They are gone, and I am going. Outside, it's snowing
just a little, just enough to make me want to think about
what a poem could be, if I turned it just right
in that light that is never there when you need it to be
I am all raw in my very cooked way. It will never be any different.
The napkins are paper as are the plates.
The tablecloth is placed over the dead and then withdrawn.
And they, too are gone, leaving only this odd little poem
riffling in space.

Mirror

My youth has left my face
it's off skateboarding
Grove street's nursing home parking lot's
hill, while all the 80 somethings watch.
What can I do? I've looked for it all day
but saw only this wrinkled man. Was he the one
who smiled at me 48 years ago
when I almost knocked him ass over end?
There's a smell of brown paper bags—
Acme's cash registers are ascending into heaven,
each checker flying off with them, and
the plaid stamps floating down from the sky.
I can hear the life I was—like, the last cricket
of the year ambushing me as I
take the garbage out. The garage door closes.
I touch my face, say let that boy alone
He's gone like all the balls he slugged
onto the rail road tracks of Fay
where the Baltimore bullet made us stop
to admire its speed. Each of us suspended
with his mitt. Let him leave. He will
hear his mother calling from the street
and answer to his name.

A Kind of Ellipsis

Whatever took off the top of your head
has left a lovely crater
Where ideas go skiing, ideas
in blue ear muffs—
What does it mean to endlessly ski
on powdered snow, leaving the
scar tissue of your life behind? We are
lonely. We ask questions, extending
the line too far—a tree line behind which the
lynx punctures the Hare's throat.
Necessity transcends the moral order.
This poem is already beyond any
trail where we started out. Thought
becomes a kind of ellipsis, a pause that is itself
a hare or a lynx or the one moving deeper
into that undiscovered country
Where already the ghosts are gathering
and not one of them speaks your name.

Waking Up

The only things solid were the pool balls
as opposed to the stripes. Everything else

was particles a swarm like bees, and one came out
to investigate me—the way a guardian drone

investigates a dark shirt, making sure it is not a bear.
You dove through me and I dove through you

After we had stopped believing in the matter at hand:
A gold watch, a night stand, boots at the threshold

of the back porch—still wearing their mud beards.
When I put my hand through time and touched

one of those cheap glass swans with the food color
dye that turned them blue or red, the "Swan" began

to shatter into space, became part of my childhood
and my 5th year floated all around me—the doilies,

my just born sister's bassinet, Mrs. Boyle next door
suspended just as Chagall suggested, the tea

an infinitely slow pouring amber, the cup a vibration
of atoms whose music I could finally hear.

Improvisation

For many years, I have known the jay
and our relations are not yet severed,
nor have I ceased to be fond of seeing
a garter snake, or a slug on an August sidewalk
or my own face—haggard though it is
yet not without its comforts—there
in an oily rainbow puddle, on the cement floor of the
Gulf Station where I am busy pumping

gas and admiring the taffeta gown that the pink
dusk clouds have sewn. I am not tired of saying
dusk and of feeling slightly weird when I say
"gloaming" (since it reminds me of Brigadoon)
I'm in the gloaming, pumping gas and hearing
I get a little bit Genghis Khan,
don't want you to get it on
with nobody else but me.

wafting through a red convertible in which two
over buffed 40 somethings with gelled hair are idling,
I am idling, too, for once not annoyed how slow
this gas pump is (it is very slow, especially in winter),
I am listening to the girl singer make the most
of Auto-tune. The next song relays how
a girl crashed her car into a bridge and doesn't care.
And I think how not caring is the Tango of cool.

I have never been cool. I have never, for example,
run a table, or popped a wheelie on a motorcycle
or rolled a joint with one hand and in the bars of
Argentina circa 1924, your fitness to mate was
judged by your tango face and ability to dance.
Damn... My mood is being wrecked. The clouds part
and the tank is full, and the gel brothers peel out
as if a convertible made you divine. And I am

lonely, as Corso said: *bereft of the bath of life.*
Or perhaps the water has grown tepid, and my skin
is shriveled. And when's the last time I made
someone go a little bit Genghis Khan?
A former student tells me that bondage between
consenting friends on Twitter is really popular—
people simulate choking, that sort of thing. I don't
have a twitter account (Facebook is for elders)

It's all controlled. It's about control.
The new sex is control and temporary solace via
control. No one is going to get strangled for real
Nothing happens without permission
It's S and M rules in a Me, too setting:
codes and permissions, and the submissive as well
as the dom gain power from their roles…
It's an America that doesn't give two shits for

Garter snakes, or the moon riding high about
the Chinese takeout. I remember Jung, that discredited
analyst, say: "Where ever love is lacking, a will to
power comes to fill the void." The convertible
goes screeching down the street, my former
student tells me: "To be able to laugh
in the face of being choked,
is empowering." I think of the peat bog bodies

found with ropes around their necks: choked, stabbed
their bones broken—all with permission.
This is nothing new. Twitter is just a peat bog,
The jays are louder than usual. A hawk must be circling
near. I am in a minivan, resisting the urge to peel
out—a soccer dad with road rage. Later that night,
some kid takes his car up to ninety on my silent street,
crashes into just the right pole to put all the power out.

Everyone is asleep in the house except my five-year-old
—her window full of red lights, and the noise
of men working at 2 o'clock—a sort of E.T. remake,
she is afraid, autistic, squeezing my hand against the
clamor. I hold her in my arms, carry her up the stairs
where my wife wakes, and Clare says: "You're a wonderful
actor. Please may I trouble you for the loan of a guinea?"
We don't know where she has heard this spiel. We laugh

lost in her perfect mimicry—the world as repeated
sound bite. *"I get a little bit Genghis Khan."* The lights
stay off until 7 the next morning. I don't sleep
but roam the dark house as if I could see, reveling
in how easily I carried my baby up the stairs, and then
back, utterly blind, her arms tight around my neck., unable to
control my tears, unable to control anything—
so in love with my daughters arms, and the barely
audible rise and fall of my sleeping son's breath.

Exercise

The world's an awful place
for those it can erase
on any given whim
beyond mere sink or swim,
those born sans might or clout
whom fortune seems to rout
daily for the sport
of seeing souls resort
to groveling on their knees
and saying *pretty please*
to some officious yawn
backed by an army's brawn.
Yet balancing with her feet,
the Bagel she should eat,
my daughter flips it twice
and catches it. Suffice
to say I stand and grin.
This moment love will win
a reprieve from all slaughter.
I love my clever daughter.

A Poem that Remembers Itself

A tepid bath—circa 1964,
sound of Flipper's theme song on the down stairs TV
I am playing with a cloth, moving it around like some
graceful eel between my knees. Skin wrinkled,
I shiver, but won't towel off until the moon through
the bathroom window comes out from its cloud.
Years later, I comfort a little kid whose dad's in Jail
by pretending a dish rag's a fish—back and forth
among the soap suds and the dishes we are washing:
the white magic of mercy—I show her the smallest
things that do not hurt, do not crush—to guard her from
her dad's forged checks, his epic bad luck.
And she loves him—with the fierce neck squeeze
of her tiny arms. There are no losers in her kingdom
I point out the stars that be planets—Jupiter riding low
over the neighbor's clothes line, Mars a feint pink
like a Junco's beak among the red and lurid lights
of the chem plants, the oil tank herds.
She lives in this vibrant chaos, an industrial sprawl:
Baway, Elizabeth, circa 1981, and the child I was is now
Twenty-thee years old, remembering the Flipper song
back when no one had died yet, no one gone to jail.
This poem remembers itself. how time is a fraud,
How I am sixty now, and moving the wash cloth
all around my giggling son, singing Flipper's song
That other child just over forty, saw me at my brother's
funeral, said she remembered me doing the fish,
how it had made her feel less sad. She says thank you.
I only have so many tricks, but they will do. I think of
Stan Laurel, and his third hand, his bowler levitating,
the feather he kept afloat above the bed as he snored.
Perhaps he has become a planet fixed over the house
of my childhood. My mother sits on the tub's curled lip,
and smokes her cig in that graceful way she had and I
watch the blue smoke curl above my cold bath, out the

window where the moon is now free and clear.
Balloon! Balloon! I heard a child cry, as if the balloon might
turn around, return to her arms. Nothing returns
It's alright, We, too, are ascending—and someone in
the kingdom of mercy is squeezing our necks—my mother
lifting me, shivering from my bath, the little girl, forty and
not well aged, my dead brother—all of it ascends
and though I will never touch those lives again they are
still in the pulse of my fingers. I close my eyes and
hum the Flipper song, see him rise out of the bay
a ball poised on his dolphin's nose ready to flip it my way—
the black and white sun of 1964, and 81
and here now, where my son is shivering in his Batman towel
Cold, the water tepid, the suds all disappeared. He hugs my
neck, this slippery seal, I kiss his wet hair, I kiss his nose.
I take him to the open window: look. There's Venus, and
there—the moon is coming out to follow us to bed.

Sassafras Leaves

For Clare

My mother dead these forty years
Two yellow mittens on her grave:
pasted there against the smooth gray stone
By an all-night rain

Part Two: A Word to the Wise

A Word to the Wise

A word:
to
the
wise   (is insufficient)
a word wizened—
increments accrued, measurable distances
and, thereby, limited, but
beyond being insufficient, what shall we be?
For what or who will we suffice?
The turtle does not lumber—not in this poem. He
measures the distance between here and here.
A word, a word for, singular and rich with possibility
a word for the wise—not to, but for,
The address is lost.
The room is vacant.
The wise, being wise, do not hear.

Here

read this:
A bizarre pattern of bridges
worms its way through
the convent of skies, and not even then
do the nuns cease praying,
washing the floors, playing:
Popular tunes, fragments of hymns
On out of tune pianos.
Where will it all end?
The bridges carry flocks of pigeons,
homeless families under
their abutments.
Everything has
been painted a bright yellow in order
to install hope. Already the spiders
are weaving their webs—parabolas to rival
the greatest feats of architecture
in the hidden eaves of Chartres.

What We Keep

for Adele

I kept a lip stick stained cigarette butt
from my mother's fancy ash tray
for ten years, transferring it from pants to pants,
to roam among my ticket stubs and rosaries—
a free ranging reminder, not of what killed her
(yes, it killed her) but of my Ma in high spirits,
a whiskey sour in her left hand, a Chesterfield in
her right, gesturing to "company", making the room
laugh, her slender arms moving to the rhythms of her
wit. She was a "howl" as they said back then,
Though I knew the other Clare, who stared out the
morning window at a dark sky, her first son
brain damaged, him, constantly rocking
in his hospital bed upstairs, him breaking the plaster walls
with fists relentlessly pounding,
him, breaking her nose when she tried to change his diaper.
I knew a hundred Clares, all funny, all stressed,
all smoking two packs a day—my childhood
a swirl of blue smoke and bobby pins,
and my brother's monthly ambulance rides.
His heart stopped forty times, and on the fortieth
she still made sure she folded our laundry, paid the bills,
over cooked the roast.
She died at fifty, a three inch hole in her face.
Her green eyes closed by a tumor that
grew in the middle of her forehead. I kept that cigarette,
not as a cautionary tale, not as some gavel to hammer down
on the damage of her addiction—but because,
I loved her, because it was nothing the world
would ever value, and that meant it was mine.
And when I finally lost it, or rather, made the mistake
of going to a dry cleaner, it was as if she'd died
again. I held those stupid pants for a long time
pulling out their pockets, absurd, lost, sniffing
for her scent

A Pastoral

*for those happy idiots in Washington who have separated parents
from children*

Here in the bucolic splendor
of Ole Nick's café, the blender
whirrs though not unpleasantly
as we drink our herbal tea.
Oh look! The sheep are passing by.
Hear them bleating? Note the cry
of the peasants proffering
madrigals; they bid us sing!
And we take the broadside then
and "tu wee, tu woo," Amen
Sing we in concordant bliss
contrapuntal, none amiss.
All is perfect. all is swell
As we ring our Ding Dong bell!
Poor and starving are elsewhere
Why, love worry, why love, care?
Prithy children torn from mothers,
fathers and assorted "others"
concern us not. We have our scones.
And our texting on smart phones:
pictures sunny. All are grinning.
Immigrants around us spinning,
take our plates. What pleasant chaps!
Happy dads in baseball caps
bounce their babies on one knee,
while they join us in our glee.
Sing Hey, ho, the wind and rain
will not touch us. We've no pain.
While authorities may pry
kids from parents. We won't cry.
We are to such fates immune.
Let us sing our happy tune!
O the green O, green O day!
While the lambs and lions lay.

Shutting Down

I want to be the last hand
that touches this light switch
and the last eyes that see the
piano before it is swallowed
up by the dark.
I love the dark but not darkness.
Ness is a towards, but dark is at.
I have no darkness in me, but
I have this dark and I want
to press my face to the air
remember when it fed my
lungs—the smell of timothy
grass, the arc of light on
leaves. What leaves is me.
I am leaving and leafing.
into some new pattern of
disarrangement. A grey will
will grasp my shoulder—hooded
figure, some comic seriousness:
shrouded—the cheap tarot of
gloomy teenagers—the Hermit
alone with his lantern, raised
I go in the dark, lit from within.
Does day light exist? Miguel
will come with me. Always
his poem ending: "Sleeping,
a man is worth the whole world."

Catbird

Wearing what, at certain angles,
appears to be a fez, the catbird
traipses amid all that stuff you haven't
cut down or back—the black
berry canes, the night shade twining
round the dwarf maples, the poison ivy
that needs to be uprooted,
all that twiggy, bushy, thorny stuff
that crap you keep intending to get to,
and get rid of but never do.
He makes the sound of a hungry cat,
or a rusty hinge, or, so a friend once swore
a porn star feigning panting ecstasy
The friend is, no doubt lying, but you
have heard catbirds mew, meow, make
a hiss, just like the sound of air
being let out of your tires. In your mind
they seem most prominent when it is
hot and humid, and sweat trickles
down the crack of your ass as you mow
the lawn. They live at the sloppy edges of
what we keep neat and trim. The suburbs
offer perfect habitat. They came with
white flight, grew bold with the birth of
joggers, and America's version of apartheid.
On the edge of the walking trails where
the low paid maintenance crew cease
to wield their weed whackers, the cat-
bird abides—chucking down a beetle or,
if it's available, a berry of poison oak.
They will shit on your freshly washed Hybrid.
Sometimes you will think you hear a baby
crying, in distress. Perhaps you are right.
Their black caps make me think of Dizzy,
cheeks puffed out, blowing a chorus of

A Night in Tunisia. I close my eyes, and
hear his horn. The salt of my sweat is in
my mouth. I have made the lawn neat
and tidy. I have enacted the lie of my nation:
all these outdoor pool tables, on which
nothing grows, except the dandelions
we are forever killing. What is a weed?
The catbird knows. And he can eat what
nearly kills us, whatever makes us sick.

Harlequin's Praise on the Feast of the Immaculate Heart of Mary

A heart immaculate was fused
with all who suffer, all who sprawl
who pratfall through the dark, who trip.
Crown her the mother of us all.

Mother of thorns, of hammer's blow,
of spear that pierced his loving side,
witness to all who spite the poor,
who trade wine's mercy in for Gall.
crown her the mother of us all.

For all whom consolation shuns
who will be butchered, martyred, cowed
for banker's profits, broker's gain,
who are pariah, outcast,, thrall
for those, like John who met Christ's eyes,
crown her the mother of us all.

And let us hear one word to turn
like leaves before a summer's rain,
one word to mark us with love's sign
that will like fire in us burn
though worldly wisdom call us vain
Doff fool's cap. Doff fool's cap and call
out, shout, *hey ho, the wind and rain.*
Crown her the mother of us all.

At a Bus Stop in El Mora, 1980

When someone tells you not to worry
and doesn't offer eternal life
or at least a good sandwich
know they are just
trying to get rid of you

in a nice way, of course, No doubt,
perhaps even with an arm squeeze
but most of the cheap forms of comfort
in this life are paper napkins close
to a raging fire.

Poof and up they go!
over the roofs of the happier neighbors.

Confronted with a brain tumor
a divorce, the death of three children
an unsightly wart—someone will
always say:

"it'll all work out" (translation: Go away)
or "God never gives us more than we can bear,"
(which means quit complaining)
or I'm so sorry (which means it's on Facebook).

If a person shows up juggling enchiladas
and fire balls for your sake,
or cleans your drain gutters and windows
or stays up all night with you as if on watch,
then it's probably not someone you expected.

The apostles fled.
The family has better things to do.
The best friend was getting laid.
Someone you hardly thought of or perhaps

didn't even like much came like Raphael
to walk the long journey with you.

Forgive your friends.
Remember family is limited (thank God)
Apostles are supposed to betray us.

Once, when I'd lost a bad job
but needed any kind of job, and was
sitting at a bus stop waiting for
the number 57 to Kenilworth, New jersey.

feeling lower than whale shit,
(and we all know where that is),
an old woman sat down beside me
and asked me why I looked so sad
and when I told her, she said: "Life crushes

us a hundred times and we are not pressed
into wine. Don't believe those idiots.
We are crushed." And she showed me the mark
of the camp, not to compete, but to let me
know there was something
behind her words,
and I said: "Forgive me. My troubles
are so small compared to yours."

And she said: "oh no. The world
makes contests. The soul does not
measure." And she kissed me on my forehead
and gave me a chicklet.

There is no moral to this story.
She was kind, like a broom sweeping
leaves in a fierce wind. She was

kind in the face of futility.
She was one who had put God
on trial for war crimes, had found God guilty
and then celebrated Shabbat.

She did not try to comfort me
or say my pain was insignificant
or promise there would be another job.
She sat with me until her bus arrived

and swallowed her whole.
And there was only the sound of traffic and my
sobbing, and I no longer knew
why I sobbed, or whether it was grief
or shame, or joy. I was rocking
like a man at the wailing wall

For all I know I was praying—
if that's what you want to call it.
It was prayer, but at the place
where praise and lamentation are both
beside the point
My heart burned like a paper plate
and it ascended. It was winter, a dirty
bus stop, and when the bus arrived
I put the change in slowly, carefully,
and stumbled to my seat.

The Flowers Offend Me Because

A Poem for the Age of Taking Offence

because they are filthy—their roots
scraggly with dirt

And the sky offends me because
it is bigger than I and how
dare that sky dwarf me?

And you offend me because…
well just because.

I think you like flowers
I think you like the sky.
You must be one of those

Sympathizers?

Beware, I have the ear of the rabbits who run the field

Their noses are atwitch to every offense.
They may look like they eat lettuce

but that's the legs of those who have offended me.

Those are the flowers. They've already eaten the sky.

Beware. Be safe! Goodbye.

Poem in Which Everyone Remembers
the Blizzard Of

Some remember the year, some the day and the year
And some just remember they had no milk and the weight

Of the snow broke that cheap little shovel the landlord had
Given them to shovel out. They remember the landlord

Later dropped dead at a Pink Floyd concert. Once in the
Middle of some pretty boring sex, they wondered exactly

Which song was playing when the landlord breathed his last.
Bad sex and blizzards don't really seem to match. It ought to

Be amazing sex considering how muted the world becomes
Just before you have to do all that shoveling, but do things

Really hang together all that often? The dark that night was
So clear you could have seen the capitol O in Orion's belt.

The snow had millions of stars twinkling in it. And some
Asshole neighbors decided to ruin the quiet with an

Overbuilt snow blower, the size of a Toyota. Drunks, young
Pretty drunks stumbled down the rutted streets and giggled

In a way that made you wish you were young and pretty and
Careless and walking in a tight jacket down a street you

Didn't live on, singing something vapid from the current hits.
Perhaps later, you'd vomit up the Vodka, but it would be

Worth it, to be surrounded by beautiful, or at least pretty
Young people wearing the sort of hats you can never again

get away with. Where were you that blizzard or the one before
that, or the one before that? All the way back to when the

Landlord handed you that shovel, and throwing it to the side
You walked half a mile, hands in pockets, to fetch the milk

and a box of mini donuts, and a tin of corned beef hash and
A loaf of rye bread. You pushed three cars out of snow banks

On your way, and two more on the return trip, the corned beef
tumbling out into the night, but you were happy to be useful

in that blizzard, in the year of the landlord, when he was still
alive—that cheap dick who, to your surprise, was a huge

Pink Floyd fan and who had a brain damaged sister he cared for
Much to your chagrin. Will everyone make you rearrange

The cosmic furniture of your contempt? Will all the souls lost
in blizzards be absolved by a sort of starry placating? Perhaps.

Perhaps the moon will come out over the closed down hospital.
Perhaps the slush prints on the supermarket floor will
Lead all pilgrims into the waiting arms of the true saints.

Wood Thrush

In the snow fields of your breast
the spirit animal of song
has left its deepest tracks.
The rest of you is rich brown red
to blend in with these dead oak leaves
where you scratch your signature
and pause after each autograph
as if to note the forest's dark approval
You live in the shade of the mature,
are for mature audiences
of two-hundred-year-old oaks, old growth—
stands that have yet to meet
a housing development, a golf course,
a bank of America.
Your song holds the liquid, languid air
of dawn and of twilight—has wandered
through centuries stopping the
most jaded woodsman until he
remembered just beyond the clearing
some unassailable thing—a passing
of a spirit animal, long extinct
Who still inhabits your minor key.
No poem rivals you, and it is best
if poets shut their mouths along
with drunk boys on a toot and
hipsters on a hike who chew their
'shrooms and wait for visions or
for sex that they regret. The world is
busy with buying and selling, yet
cousin to the loquacious Robin, you
move as a spirit moves, heard
far more deeply than ever seen,
already gone in the way that all
things beautiful seem already gone,
lovely for their fleeting, or perhaps

as Rilke said: You who never
arrived.
Your song is enough. Dayenu!
Even if we had only heard you when
we'd forgotten we were, ourselves,
a kind of prayer, even if all else had been
broken in us, blighted and betrayed

This would have been enough:
to hear you at our beginning, at
our end: leaf scratcher, thrush, your
potbellied, puffed up body hidden
in the shade of some dark forest canopy
singing everything we have ever lost,
everything that is worth our grieving.

Part Three: Post-Pastoral

The Three-toed Rhyme

A Riddle

The willow has no cause
except what we impugn
to it—a cause for grief,
a weeping, (call it woe).

A troglodyte might live
as well there as a cave,
as backwards in its shade
as any three-toed rhyme

In Another Life

In another life, a car passes me by.
It's filled with all those I have failed to love (It's a big car).
I start running after it, shouting: "Hey, I'm sorry."
The shout repeated often. Panting, running out of gas,
I begin to
wonder if I really mean it. If I don't, then why shout?
Why put on this suit of ash, why beat myself over the head
with a Louisville slugger? Why indeed?
The car's license plate reads: Failed to love us 448.
It is about to turn the corner.
I sit down on the curb and give it the bird, raise my
finger to its exhaust pipe. A few leaves drift over the
street. Otherwise it's a cul de sac—one of those
pleasant enough neighborhoods, where one guy starts
blowing his leaves, and the next follows until an army
of leaf blowers are busy drowning out whatever
we need to drown. I'm breathing heavily.
Chasing regret is a loser's past time. Why did I need
to love them? Some guy comes over
says: Hey buddy, where's your house?
He hands me a beer and starts speaking of the beer's
pedigree, where it was crafted, what flavors are
ghosted in its otherwise pilsner bite.
I take a sip. Not bad. He says: Hey, dude, where's
your leaf blower? Good question.
Wait a minute he says and he goes into his garage
comes out a minute later
producing a real beauty and another beer.
A house starts spinning down from the sky, just like
all the other houses, and complete with a lawn that
needs some major leaf blowing. I say thanks
and get to work. I have failed to love anyone.
I'm not sure who or where my wife and kids are but,
no doubt

they will appear soon, too—wanting loans, better
communication skills,
more Triple A coverage. Until then I rev that baby up!
I am herding piles and piles of dead leaves.
I got the rhythm down solid. I sing "get along lil doggies!"
Part of me wants to weep into the stars
and another part of me wants to
jam it hard into someone from behind.
I guess that combination makes me American.
I'm American. Whatever love demands, it is beyond my
frail capacities, but that's ok. There's a bit of chill in the air.
Later, Georgia or Notre dame will be facing off.
Someone's helmet will flash gold in the sunlight.
I'll have blown every leaf off my lawn but I'll keep an eye
out and if, one of them sneaks onto my property
I'll take out my AK47, as is my right, and blast that intruder
into Smithereens

Post-Pastoral

In Memory of Maxine Kumin

They were there: four thousand types of blackbird:
Starlings, grackles, cowbirds, and, well, red polls
All devouring the weed heads, the tender shoots
of timothy grass, and crab grass, and dandelion
seeds, and... you get my drift: a shit load of birds;

and who am I not to be amazed? But I called to the
family of my familiars: look, a murmuration has
landed in the yard! They are eating their own
reflections in the wading pools of the recent rain
Ten thousand black birds in the glistening grass!

But everyone (and this included attractive, fairly
Intelligent people) just kept doing whatever it is
they do with their days. It was as if I spoke gibberish,
until I hit them with balled wads of paper, then cash
and they turned and said: "oh yes." Which upset me
more than perhaps I wanted to admit. It is difficult to

share an enthusiasm for certain sudden phenomena.
We are all trying to keep connected through the veil
Of the text, but it gets away from us, and we lose our
Stupidity. Will no one be made stupid, beautifully so—
Knocked Senseless by the vast flock of black birds

Feeding on the glistening flora, in the cold wind
of an early Spring day? (a long silence followed by:
Don't you see we are busy buying and selling and
Deciding whether or not the new bar is worth trying
Tonight if only for their mixed drinks? Don't be a drag).

But I am a drag, I am a sturm und drang. I am something
In German. I can just feel the weight of the black forest
Pulling me away from my normal activities I would
formerly enjoy. There is a lawn full of black birds, damn
it, and someone besides me ought to care about the

gathering. The reader has no doubt stopped reading,
has realized this poem has broken the fourth wall and
perhaps even the fifth and is weighed down by the
twee playfulness of a poet not qualified to speak properly
of blackbirds at all. But why must I be qualified? I went to

the window and saw the vast flock in the glistening grass
and saw how they chattered, snatching and flapping,
rapacious yet charming in their violent way, completely
oblivious to me or my stupefied gaze, my amazement
that caused me to give constant cry: Look! Hey Look! You

Spawns of Satan! Look… but to no avail until I
Broke free of the window and out the door and
spun wildly in their midst until the midst flew up
And I flew up with them—a Red poll! The sunflower
Seeds falling from my vanishing pockets: glistening
like ebony gods beside a discarded shovel: my final gift.

An Old Vaudevillian Dream

A tremor in my hand
back bent, a name's erased,
recovered as I stand
two hours past misplaced;
and that same flight of stairs
I took once at a bound
now troubles me to sigh.
My heart will surely pound
and beat hard for an hour
or even, perhaps, stop.
I quip: "I'm mountaineer!"
and, stumble to the top.
The rueful, panting "done"
I shout to no one's ear
"I've climbed this stairwell, Lord."
(It only took a year.)
I laugh against the pain
that murmurs in my chest.
Don't wake it up. Be still
achieve a good night's rest.
but slumbering, I dream
of balancing on a limb
across a river's flow.
I know I cannot swim.
Yet caught between my fear
and my futility
I leap into mid-air
and pratfall to one knee.

Winter Poem

To rub the sweet gum's leaf base and the winter green
twigs of yellow birch—to crush God into scent
might for an hour heal the sting and taint
of human effort—like a sacrament
made wholly out of what the wind has tossed,
this litter down, the detritus of twigs.
When all has come to nothing, this remains:
Snow fresh stink of root rust, mountain ash—
dried fruits like keys some sorrow has misplaced
wind-kind, this blistered bark's ferocity
and fallen timber—broken arms of the white pine
twisted limbs of poplar. the gnarled trunk
of a silver maple brought down to the frozen river bank
to wait the thawed current that will drag it in

The Compound Sentence

By the time you read this missive, this heal-all
this sentence of wrought iron
hewn from whatever will
suffice—a cure for what ails ye
your lungs and lethargy,—
whatever phlegm or flimflam has effaced

your noble visage and made you
a continent bereft

of spirit, a sea becalmed, still
stinking of that putrid stillness
that so troubles active men
making them petition God
For head winds ,

Whatever ill- fated being lurks,
it shall be vanquished;

and then you will know the power
Of compound sentences.
And every tear will be wiped from your
eyes. It will all be clear

Clear as after a fog
has lifted And you stand there looking
over a vast expanse of stuff:
Malls, diners, over passes, highway signs

And you say: that's sure a lot of
stuff. Jesus. It's a mess.
And yet are pleased by the sheer weight
of it—the pulse of its being.

The Kingdom of Broken Necks

The giraffe must slip and break its neck
This is the law of rain and of reflection.
The giraffe thinks he has a rival
For his affections
When all he has is himself
Reconfigured on the wet concrete floor
There's a longing that knows no peace.
The neck is too ambitious
And must, as in Chekhov's universe,
go off in act three
or, rather break, as the camera cuts
To a little boy dressed as a giraffe
Who is playing Fur Elise at a quicker
Pace than is usually indicated.
The metronome is hidden in
The northern lights. It demands
An end to subterfuge and excess
rubato. It likes things neat. It likes
notes clipped. The child slips in
a part of the piece that often graces
cheap wine commercials. The soft
gaslight of another century suggests
He was born to the wrong years.
What is he to do? He bangs his
Forehead against the keys: the perfect
Child is there—the one who can save
The world and is waiting for him not
To screw up, but he always hits a
Wrong note. The violence of failure
 is not part of the metronome's decree:
dead child, dead giraffe. How many have
succumbed to the longing for perfection?
Under the gaslight, Ingrid Berman smiles.
It's an old movie his teacher loves.
There is a light in which only accident

may hold us—just so, just right,
a place where the metronome stops
and rapture begins: slow enough that
We might catch our breaths, manage
not to die—that place where the rain
is falling softly, and softly falling,
a slip of the pen or the fingers that
makes all things possible.

The Puddle Jumper

Before anyone turns my father into an abuser (that's my job as the writer, not yours), I want to mention that he worked a 3:30 to 12, sometimes till 2 am shift in a paper factory, came home, and got up at 7 to take me to my little league game. He was a semi-pro baseball player, a catcher (A very short but agile one) who batted .336 his last year in a fast pitch softball league (he was 42).

My father never forced me to play, He never humiliated me for my decided lack of co-ordination He never took over the coach's duties. He'd watch. When his opinion was called for, he gave it. The 18-year-old red haired kid named Tommy who coached us didn't know what he was doing. Rocky (my dad) would play his bench coach. When none of the mothers would allow their son's to catch (we had one pitcher. Donny Maholovich, who was fast, wild, and seemed to have a talent for breaking his catcher's thumbs) my dad said to me: "Are you willing to catch, kid?" I said: "Sure." I loved saying sure. It's a word you drag along like a stick across a chain link fence—a long, diphthong of a word. Years later I was delighted when I found out the poet Delmore Schwartz had written a poem called "the Great American Word sure."

So, I caught. Donny threw one fast ball just as the sun, the shadow of the swinging bat, and my decided lack of ability all converged. The ball hit me in the eye and knocked me out for a few seconds. Later, after a visit to the emergency room, my dad took me out to a diner, told me I could order anything on the menu which, as in all jersey dinners weighed more than some toddlers, and he said: "I'm proud of you. You don't have a lot of talent, but you have something better: you got balls. kid. Don't tell your ma I said that."

This was my father., It was also my father when I was teased and called a faggot for using the word lovely and for writing poems. He told me about a kid in his neighborhood who was always practicing the violin and all the kids gave him a rough time. Years later, the kid ended up a violinist in the NBC radio orchestra and all the kids who called him names were pushing brooms, digging ditches or toiling in a factory. This story was borrowed (I think), but still it helped. His point was he didn't want me to stop using the world lovely and he wrote poems, too, albeit, more like graffiti:

When I was a wee wee tot
they sat me down on that cold, cold pot
and made me wee, wee whether
I wanted to or not
(merry Christmas)

When anyone had a fever, my dad was the best at drawing it out. When I cheered a little too loudly at a basketball game, a man clouted me hard on my ear and said: "pipe down you little bastard.". My father very calmly threw a right cross and knocked the guy out on the bleacher. This was in the sixties when things like this didn't go viral or anywhere at all, and all the cops at the game knew my dad from his diamond gloves days. They knew he never hit anyone unless the guy deserved it. My dad helped the man up, brushed his coat off, and said: " Listen. You ever hit my son or any kid again, I'll make sure your bully ass is in the hospital." The guy left. No one sued. End of that story.

My father had grown up on Staten Island, in Princess Bay, which, even in the depression 30's, was a rough place. He went to Curtis high for a while where they once broke up a ten-thousand-dollar crap game. Boxing had helped keep him out of jail., and, as an amateur, he'd won some championship bouts. He was a bantam weight then. By the time I knew him he was a light weight—all muscle and fast. This was the father I worshiped. Now for the other guy who will make the reader breathe on and polish up the word, abuser.

My father was a puddle jumper. That's someone who doesn't drink every day, but when he does drink, he dives into it. At least twice a year, my dad's puddle turned into a lake and he sank to the bottom only to resurface as a mean drunk. He'd come stumbling home and insist we all eat the cold white castle burgers he'd brought with him. We'd be asleep. My mother's protestations lead to him waking us from our sleep, marching us down into the kitchen and forcing us to eat three white castles a piece. I loved white castles but not at 2 in the morning, with my father breathing booze all over me, and telling me I was a cry baby. "You're lucky I'm not like my father." He'd say. "you're lucky you don't get a belt buckle across your kisser."

My dad never hit me across the kisser. He never hit me when he was drunk. He never hit my mother, but the menace was always there. He could make a belt snap. His own father had come home and taken the buckle to his face. He still had the scars. He never hit my mom, but Christmas was always tense. It was on Christmas of 1939 that his aunt and Uncle had told him they were not his parents and that the people he'd been calling aunt Bertha and uncle James were his real folks. It was that Christmas that he was taken away from a home he loved and made to live with his "real parents" one of whom was a coast guard captain (his dad) and a mean drunk who drank every day: schnapps. Lots of schnapps. To the day he died, my father could not stand the smell of schnapps. All I know is my mother would tell us: "Your father had a rough childhood. If he gets cranky at Christmas, that's why. You have to pray for him."

It was Christmas of 1939 when my dad's world fell apart, and Christmas of 1964 when my world was temporarily upended.

The transformation of good dad into drunk always began with a certain look on his face. His face would look as if he were peering into some deep troubling crystal and not liking it. He'd start pacing. Sometimes, he'd insist the television was too loud and he couldn't hear himself think, or that my mother hadn't cleaned the kitchen to spec. He was looking to pick a fight. This Christmas eve, after cursing the lights, and cursing the decorations, and making us shut off the Christmas carols because they made him want to cut his wrists, he looked at my socks: I had one black and one brown sock on. I thought they were close enough. He looked and then he said: "Did your mother do that?" I was six. I said: "No... I know how to put my socks on." My dad said: "if there's one thing I can't stand, its carelessness goddamn it. You're old enough to know the goddamned difference between a brown and a black sock." He made me go upstairs and match the socks. And then my mother said:" you're being a little rough on him" My father said: "Rough? You're turning him into a goddamned spoiled brat. You're letting him think there are no rules damn it. What kind of kid puts on one black and one brown sock? What kind of dumb shit is that?" And then he said: "I'm going for a walk.". We all knew what that meant.

Eight hours later. he came stumbling home. My brother and I always slept in the same room when my dad "went for a walk." My brother, John told me pretend it was all a movie—no matter what went down. We heard stuff crashing We heard:". "Just a bunch of ungrateful kids and a frigid ass wife." We heard: " Hey kids, come on down stairs. I got some Smoked whiting for you! Join your frigid mother!" We heard our mom say: "Rocky, you're drunk. Go to bed." "I'll tell you when I'm drunk," he said and we heard the glass Swan that was a feature of all houses we knew smash into the wall, painting it with food coloring. Next we heard: "That's my tree! I paid for it and I can chuck it out the window If I feel like it. Hey kids get up and have some smoked whiting!"

My dad opened the window. That was lucky because, in his state of drunkenness, he could have just chucked the tree through the glass. he opened the window and threw the tree out onto the porch. He went out onto the porch and started calling out to the neighbors: "And if you don't like it, I'll lick every one of you."

Someone must have called the cops and, of course, my mom called Aunt Elizabeth, who, no matter what, always came in her large green Chevy with the fins (A 1961 model, the newest in all the family) and picked us up. She'd never married. She said this was because she had better sense than her siblings. We would put my brain damaged bother Peter in the middle, so he wouldn't rock too much and break the windows. I was on one side of him and my brother John on the other, all of us tucked under blankets. My sister, a year and a couple months old, was in the front seat nestled in my mother's arms. Aunt Elizabeth adjusted her rhinestone glasses. She swallowed a cough drop. "We're going to get another tree. "She announced cheerfully. "Let's put on the Christmas carols and sing."

The cops did not arrest my father. he was known as a good boxer, as a supporter of the PAL. One of them took him to sleep it off in his basement. We picked out a tree at Josephix lot on Bayway. We all said it was better than the tree we'd had. We were lying, but it was an agreed upon lie. We stopped at George's famous hot dogs for Hot dogs and hot chocolate. I was crying for fifteen minutes, but then, finally, my brother gave me the barber's itch, a sort of noogy, and whispered: "You sound like a horse while they're cutting his balls off." That made me giggle. My mother remarked from the front seat: "What did I hear you say, John Peter Weil?" My brother said: "I said merry Christmas Ma. "I'll give you merry Christmas Ma." She said. And then Bing Crosby sang Silent Night.

We came back and took the balls and lights off the old tree, we left the tree on the porch, somehow the smoked whiting had shaken loose from their newspaper wrapping and I spied three fish heads, eyes glimmering in the dark from the branches. We put the lights and the balls that weren't broken on the new tree. My father was gone. Wherever he was, he was probably passed out and snoring— we hoped without a cigarette.

The next day, my dad came home. Nothing was said. I looked at him for a long minute. I looked down at my socks. They matched. He came over and knelt in front of me. He tousled my hair. He hugged me. "I'm sorry." He said. My brother John said: "you were really shit faced last night. You were an idiot." He was challenging my dad, letting him

81

know he didn't forget. He forgave, but he didn't forget, and he was challenging my father—all four feet eleven inches and ten years of him. My father said: "hey... watch your language... who told you you could say shit?" My brother answered: "Santa told me after he got shit faced and threw the tree out the window." My father looked at the two of us and hunched his shoulders. Then he said: "What's done is done.". My mother came in from the kitchen, holding my baby sister and a bottle. "Are you proud of yourself?" she said. "You made quite a show for the neighbors." He said: "I'll never throw a tree out the window again Clare, I promise. I'm so sorry."

He kept his word. he never threw a tree out the window again. He did get drunk at my cousin Betty's wedding and end up causing a fuss. His puddles became less frequent until my mother died. When she was dying, he worked all day (he got on the day shift) then drove his car up to St Barnabas hospital and sat with her for hours, holding her hand. I went with him most of the time except when he'd go early, and I was still in school. He looked lost during her illness. Shell shocked. One day, I got a ride from my friend Jimmy to the hospital. This was about three weeks before my mother died. She had a huge hole in her face both from the mouth cancer and from the experimental chemo which led eventually to gangrene (they had told her it was one of the possible side effects). My father sat there in his Whitestone products uniform, a pair of reading glasses he and my mom shared perched on his nose, patiently, gently, with his good coordination, painting my mother's toe nails. I asked him why he was doing that. he said: "She's my girl." He started crying. He pressed his face into my gut.

I didn't know how to hold my father. I grabbed him in a head lock. To a modern person, especially a middle-class person, he's an abuser. I won't say he wasn't, but he was also someone I loved and who loved me. And at that moment, he was some fifty-year-old man sobbing into his 18-year-old son's St Mary's uniform. He shuttered. He scared the shit out of me. I said to him: "you sound like a horse in the middle of having his balls cut off." It didn't make him giggle the way it had when my brother said it.

I don't think he even heard me. I held on to his head as tight as I could. I stared at his bald spot. The glasses fell to my feet. My mother, out of it on morphine, said: "be still Rocky. Be still. It will all come home." It will all come home was an expression of her mother's. I remembered my grandmother saying it whenever my brother Peter, my brain damaged brother would be rushed to the hospital with his convulsions. It will all come home. Eventually my dad, stopped crying. I let loose my grip. Jimmy had excused himself to the nurse's station and then split. My parents watched the news together. We watched Happy Days. The Fonz could snap his fingers and make reality do his will. We didn't have that power. Jimmy had gone home. My dad drove me back to Elizabeth. It had started to snow hard and my mother, weeks away from her death, was worried about us getting down the steep hill upon which Barnabas sat. We drove through the snow, silent for the most part. My dad said: "I know you think we didn't love each other. What do you know? I'm sorry. it's my fault. Its all my fault." A minute went by, and I said: "Nah. dad. It's not all your fault ... maybe sixty-eight percent of it is your fault." He laughed. He reached over and touched my head from the driver's seat. He said: "I got a little wise ass here. You want a cough drop? "I said: "Sure."

Anadiplosis

There is a place
a place with which I am all too familiar,
familiar yet from which I am estranged
estranged as from most places except
this is familiar, like a ridge of scar tissue
where some brilliant surgeon has cut
cut neatly, with great deliberation then closed
it up—the it that contains the absence
of whatever needed to be removed.
Removed from most things, I wonder
if I am not a vestige organ,
something, the function of which has
ceased to exist, yet can still rot in the body,
can still become the unwanted and
perhaps deadly element that must be
excised. I have removed myself
from the scene of the accident. I am sure
sure there was an accident here,
here where the chickory closes up and
the other weeds weed around for
God knows what—a stiff wind? Here it
comes, a stiff wind, moving through
bull thistle, and flea bane, and queen Anne's lace.
This place, this place has memories.
Even if they were mine, I would walk right
through them as if they were someone else's
This phantom limb—whose is it?
I keep waking up in pain and I have two
limbs, the usual number. Who died and
left me boss of an all-pervasive agony?
Good question. My whole being
must answer it: you, and you, and you, and you
come to the window, the one with the pretty
curtains, and say: I wish you well.
Even if you don't mean it, I will be grateful

as I am even now for the smallest favors—
this blue day flower for instance, that pushes up
through a crack in the side walk, and
not as hope, but as a species of Herbaceous
weed originally from East Asia

Paradise Lost

In the Life we lead, every Paradise is lost.
—Robert Hass

I used to take people to paradise—
A polish/ Portuguese restaurant
serving steaming bowls of
Kale garlic soup and Borscht.
It's closed now, with dark leaves
scuttling across its blighted
Portico. On the broken window
a sample menu hangs itself
reminding us that two plosives
once comprised a sort of bliss
that could be lifted gently on
a spoon, the blessed lips giving
it a gentle blow until it cooled.
Down the block, they have a
store where you can order
things without making any human
contact. There is one clerk to
oversee the processing of goods.
She looks tired, her eye lids heavy
as a giant sea turtle's. Where will
she lay her eggs? And what birds
of progress will come to ravish them?
There are holes in all the living.
How will we hatch? Is that sea we
are frantically paddling toward
a sea? Will the drones pick us off
Leaving us gutted in the sand?
Surely, We will see a better day
when all the riff raff have been jailed
or made to work as unpaid interns.
Until then I tell her the mustard
dispenser is broken, She calls the
Manager, He asks me for my

degree, has me fill out a ten page
survey, marks my forehead with a star.
He reaches into his coat and
produces four mustard packets.
I leave the store, another satisfied
customer. The Drone waves a gloved
Mickey Mouse hand from two feet above
my head. It drops a flyer at my feet.
I can't read it. My eyes are on strike.
Soon, law enforcement will come,
calling my sight an unlawful assembly.
They will pluck forth my eyes and tie
me to the temple's pillar.
Until then, I am remembering
the smell of paradise. It was long
ago. The garlic was thick or thin
depending on who was at the stove
thin as the veil of the covenant:
translucent, something. you could
peer through all the way to Gilad.
I touch my finger to my brow,
remember borscht, remember sour cream.
It was a dream. The star is rising
from the steam of my own breath.
This progress is so bland. so let us
season it with just a pinch of death.

Why is it Always December Between us?

Why is it always December between us?
It's dark. Wind blows through all the cracks.
We skate on breaking ice. We dare to drown.
The snowmen leer, then melt. We bear our deaths
In every syllable we speak. Dig out the broken
Toys beneath the snow, We save what we desire.
But what is that? Desire? I knew it once so long ago
A long, long time ago, before we died,
Or is it our breaths waned, and dwindled down
Until no day could find us whispering a breath
Against the glass? Why breathe? Why dispel
The daylight withering on those icy boughs.
We once called arms? A deepening begins
Drifts over us, beneath us. Winter wins.

A Small Thing

I thought I saw you in the museum
your body
looked like a buoy. We were part
of a calm misunderstanding
like sunlight on a bottle cap
a small thing
Falling into the dark where
the cliffs really are,
the blind, reddening stars

Poem in Which I Shit on Unity

after the election

I don't want to come together.
I don't even agree with myself.
There's parts of me
even now, in Outer Mongolia
cursing over a cup of Kumis
and other parts riding the
back of a neutrino through
the center of a Trump sign.
I pass like a ghost through Latvia
I am an Embryo curled
in the womb of a hot house Tulip.
There are those who want me
born so they can shoot me
legally later—(when I deserve it).
I am frost. I am fire and all four
winds pulling at the plastic strip
of this crime scene. I am told
today about a poem in which
Three pissed off plant workers
in Michigan beat a Chinese man
to death, thinking him Japanese.
This was long ago, when Toyota
was kicking America's ass. I
wonder if they said: "Oops"
or "close enough" I wonder if
the moon is the same for
everyone just after, and nothing
nothing tilts or falls in grief
from the sky.

Early Winter

From the half-rotten ash-tree's topmost twig,
a mottled cloud dives—and all the ash keys quiver,
while out a little further, a murmuration
rises and falls upon the freezing river.
I join my own reflections to the geese
whose victory v moves from the river's edge
and skyward, a broken circle of rosary beads
vanishes. A blue jay takes the pledge
of his own name. Such a wild crested bird
must have a reason to the riot in his rhyme:
and then I see the red-tailed hawk that rides
on thermals, wings spread, how peacefully it glides
then drops—a thousand feet to snatch a hare.
I bite my lip and bleed into its cry.

Grey from Grey

The beasts lie down to rest
and heaven lies down as well
and where the sky or sea begin
no human eye can tell
unless a cloud or wave
inform, delineate
the border between sea and sky
or soul parse grey from grey.

Before Another Snow

Cardinal in a world gone monochrome,
gone grey, gone white, divested of what's red,
I leave six wedges of a ripe blood orange
to see you though the storm, to see me through.
There isn't much an aging man can do,
but watch things fall, and fall himself at times
toward revelry, toward what will not suffice
to nourish him. I have no sage advice,
past love, past caring, past my feeble rhymes,
I long for something I can never name,
and seeing you, my blood still stirs, still flows
red against the losses I have born.
So thanks to you, who give no thanks to me
except to be, to be, to be enough.

Glass Swan Full of Food Coloring

In Memory of My Grandmother

It's late in the day and the French window's dust
is charged with light
There's a swan preening its glass blown breast,
heavy bottom filled with aquamarine food coloring.

Why? What sort of tacky try at beauty this?
And yet the smell of too heavy
Mahogany, the china closet with its dishes
all showing happy Germans (or are they Swiss?)
Playing leap frog, strangely moves me.

It's hard to watch my childhood become extinct.
The Joan Crawford Coca-Cola tray on which
my long dead Aunt carried out her finest cheese
Is worth, perhaps, a fin

I'm not selling anything. It's all in the mind—
The inventory of a man turning sixty: three stents,
a sudden clenching of the heart at night
That brings me to my knees.

As a kid I was always tempted to drink the water.
It looked like Kool-Aid. The swans, the doilies
The upright piano that only I cared to play…

It will all go one night when my brain clicks off.
I think about being Caruso, consider singing
a high Note so pure, the glass swan shatters into God.
I dream a single snow flake falls and
Touches it just so and sets the food dye running—

A deluge, a cataclysm. But that's all one, Terrified,
I sit in the dark, and go over it all in my head.
remembering the woodblock slightly cracked—
A piano on which you dare not play any thirds.

Bare fifths sufficed. The Swan shook whenever
I and my cloddish cousins ran past it at play,
trembled as the leaping Germans did. The whole
House shook with our laughter. And now?
My hand shakes placing the nitro under my tongue,
my children asleep beyond the world of Swans.

Compline

Come touch this wind
Out of a vagrant longing
that stands through the night in the house of the dawn
Lift up your chalice with worn mumbled prayers
And sing to ghosts.
May the hour genuflect praise
And deepen the dark river's gaze
That holds the trees and houses accountable
To whatever they shelter.
It is this residue in things
this now, that abides with us,
that gives us bread, our daily bread
to break

Postlude: A Little Hope

A Round of Sorts

Someday I won't be here
but I insist the gnarled linden trees
on certain streets will be a little taller
still giving off their scent come June,
and some young boy
in love and maybe slightly drunk
will trip on an uneven tree root,
be pressed against a
trunk with kissing, and not even
know it's a Linden, not know
its the Linden flowers and not her
body that makes this scent:
or maybe it was her body, all that is
grown outward into the invisible
so that years after that night has fled
something in June will remind him
life was often kind, often ecstatic,
that it was scented and dappled by what
he could never name. Someday
when I am no longer here.

On the Feast of the Assumption

Like any ascent, she left a wake
The flowers needed time to settle down,
The grasses, and leaves as well
Until there was nothing to prove
A host of angels had carried her away—
Not a hair or a head out of place.
Two thousand years later, she
Keeps re-appearing, never to the
Obvious suspects: not to Bishops, nor
to chemists, nor to the "deserving"
Throngs, let's say, the Catholic writer's
Seminar at AWP? She has a thing for
Lowliness, so that the smarter set
often smiles—a vague and friendly
grin (they're made for better tropes)
And leave her to old ladies with spotted
Hands, to men who have the shakes
To those in the dark who can still say
Have mercy on me, a poor sinner.
She who never sinned is their chief friend,
The one who causes constantly a cry
Hail full of grace! Star of the sea,
Arc of the covenant. The grass bends
For a moment, then returns to
Its upright pose. children wake
From their trance. Neurologists
Peel back whatever brain leaves may
Get them to the heart of all this
Nonsense—the thousands in some
Mud field watching the rain cease
And the sun spin, then dance, then
Drop. Yet it is no trick, no miracle
That raises her above the angels
But only the soft word yes, and the
Quiet persistent light slanting
Through her Bedroom window.

New Year Day Marigold Poem

At two below, but with the sun
a bright orange/yellow disk
I greet the new year!

And why not exclamation points?
And why not this marigold which
I can easily conjure

By taking a wide palate knife
covered in a thick smudge of
orange/yellow paint and press

deep into the canvas of my day
impasto and—. walla!
Calendula officinalis! My dear friends

The inflorescences of which
I am assured
are truly yellow, comprising

a thick capitulum or flowerhead
4 to 7 centimeters in diameter
surrounded by two rows of hairy bracts;

Oh Hairy bracts! yon guardians
of the sun! The Green man's
nose is holly berry red

his shadow lengthens on
the back yard lawn—a white blue shield
embossed with cat prints, coon prints,

little Junco jots, the hemlocks
taking bows—the ideograms
of some great joy of which I am aware

for it pleases me to play
the thrush, my white beard hanging from
a haggard face like Spanish moss

On the cusp of sixty,
I sing my marigold song, I would
both thrush and marigold join

in a prophecy of green
a child, bundled up—a fat little pear!
with shorts arms waving

beneath the rattling locust pods
at his mother ten feet away.
The fruit we are told, is

a thorny curved achene;
for something sharp must make
so great a fire.

Praise the marigold! Strike flint
against the Christmas greens.
In the deep sting

of two below, I open
my black coat and spin
beneath the hemlock trees,

a figure in orange/yellow light
my soul, a white smoke risen
Te Deum Laudamus! to greet the
coming year.

The New York Quarterly Foundation, Inc.

New York, New York

Poetry
Magazine

Since 1969

Edgy, fresh, groundbreaking, eclectic—voices from all walks of life.

Definitely NOT your mama's poetry magazine!

The *New York Quarterly* has been defining the term contemporary American poetry since its first craft interview with W. H. Auden.

Interviews • Essays • and of course, lots of poems.

www.nyq.org

No contest! That's correct, NYQ Books are NO CONTEST to other small presses because we do not support ourselves through contests. Our books are carefully selected by invitation only, so you know that NYQ Books are produced with the same editorial integrity as the magazine that has brought you the most eclectic contemporary American poetry since 1969.

Books

www.nyq.org

poetry at the edge™

CPSIA information can be obtained
at www.ICGtesting.com
Printed in the USA
LVHW050438200723
752910LV00008B/423